A Crabtree Roots Book

Un libro de Las Raíces de Crabtree

TEACHER
MAESTRO

DOUGLAS BENDER

Traducción de Pablo de la Vega

People I Meet
La gente que conozco

Crabtree Publishing

crabtreebooks.com

School-to-Home Support for Caregivers and Teachers

This book helps children grow by letting them practice reading. Here are a few guiding questions to help the reader with building his or her comprehension skills. Possible answers appear here in red.

Before Reading:

- What do I think this book is about?
  - *This book is about teachers.*
  - *This book is about what a teacher does at work.*

- What do I want to learn about this topic?
  - *I want to learn where a teacher works.*
  - *I want to learn what a teacher does.*

During Reading:

- I wonder why...
  - *I wonder why some people become teachers.*
  - *I wonder why teachers use chalkboards.*

- What have I learned so far?
  - *I have learned that some teachers work in classrooms.*
  - *I have learned that teachers help people learn.*

After Reading:

- What details did I learn about this topic?
  - *I have learned that teachers can teach many different subjects.*
  - *I have learned that not all teachers teach in classrooms.*

- Read the book again and look for the vocabulary words.
  - *I see the word **classroom** on page 6, and the word **board** on page 8. The other vocabulary words are found on page 14.*

This is a **teacher**.

Él es un **maestro**.

A teacher helps people.

Un maestro ayuda a la gente.

This teacher is in a **classroom**.

Este maestro está en un **aula**.

abcdefgh

A teacher writes on a **board**.

Los maestros escriben en un **pizarrón**.

1 2 3 4 5 6 7 8 9 10

A teacher sits at a **desk**.

Los maestros se sientan en un **escritorio**.

Do you know a teacher?

¿Conoces a algún maestro?

Words to Know
Palabras para conocer

classroom
aula

board
pizarrón

teacher
maestro

desk
escritorio

31 Words

This is a **teacher**.

A teacher helps people.

This teacher is in a **classroom**.

A teacher writes on a **board**.

A teacher sits at a **desk**.

Do you know a teacher?

33 Palabras

Él es un **maestro**.

Un maestro ayuda a la gente.

Este maestro está en un **aula**.

Los maestros escriben en un **pizarrón**.

Los maestros se sientan en un **escritorio**.

¿Conoces a algún maestro?

People I Meet

TEACHER

La gente que conozco

MAESTRO

Crabtree Publishing

crabtreebooks.com 800-387-7650

Written by: Douglas Bender
Translation by: Pablo de la Vega
Designed by: Rhea Wallace
Series Development: James Earley
Proofreader: Ellen Rodger
Educational Consultant: Christina Lemke M.Ed.
Production manager: Candice Campbell
Photographs: Shutterstock: ESB Professional: cover; michaeljung: p. 1, 3, 14; wavebreakmedia: p.5; Monkey Business Images: p. 7, 13, 14; Evgeniy Kalinovskiy: p.9, 14; Szasz-Fabian Illka Erikca: p. 10-11, 14

Published in Canada
Crabtree Publishing
616 Welland Ave.
St. Catharines, Ontario
L2M 5V6

Published in the United States
Crabtree Publishing
347 Fifth Avenue,
Suite 1402-145
New York, NY, 10016

Library and Archives Canada Cataloguing in Publication
Available at the Library and Archives Canada

Library of Congress Cataloging-in-Publication Data
Available at the Library of Congress

Paperback: 9781039624634
Ebook: 9781039625471
Epub: 9781039625051

Printed in the U.S.A./CP122025